CLASSIC MARQUES

Horse and Steam Trams of Britain

DAVID GLADWIN

NOSTALGIA ROAD

Nostalgia Road 2016

Front cover: Leeds Tramways Co No 58, an Eades reversible car, recorded at the Headingley terminus in about 1890.

Rear cover top: Brand new and gleaming, this Gateshead & District Tramways Co trailer is very skeletal but, like many others of the period, was designed to weigh under four English tons. The details are fascinating: the longitudinal 'outside' seating; the lack of 'decency' (advertising) boards; safety staircases; and, mohair curtains (these were soon dispensed with as they became infested). Built and supplied by the Falcon Engine & Car Co in 1883, later illustrations show this class of vehicle as having a slotted-in cover upstairs, decency boards and other changes. The dimensions were 19ft 4in in length (27ft 6in over the buffers), 5ft 4½in in width and 13ft 0in in height; seating capacity was 52.

A CIP record for this book is available from the British Library

ISBN 9781908 347114

Rear cover bottom: Nos 19 and 20 were built by Thos Green & Son and delivered to Huddersfield Corporation Tramways in 1891. These were excellent vehicles, albeit rather heavy on coke apparently; as compound working was unusually employed, they were driven by hand-picked drivers. Cylinders were 9 x 14in on the high-pressure side and 14 x 14in on the low. The tubes on the roof are Blackburn designed; these involved passing the steam from cylinders, etc through pipes inside these annular tubes — probably the most efficient design ever. The trailer was built by Geo F Milnes. Lifeguards are fitted to the engine and to the trailer, although the latter were rarely photographed, and the engine is here being watered.

Printed in Malta by Melita Press

**Nostalgia Road is an imprint of
Crécy Publishing Limited**
1a Ringway Trading Estate
Shadowmoss Road
Manchester M22 5LH

www.crecy.co.uk

Acknowledgements

First and foremost Gerald Hartley for allowing the use of some tiny part of his collection of images of tramway company crests. Members of the Tramway & Light Railway Society and Light Rail Transit Association who have added bricks to the wall of knowledge. I'd also like to thank following: Editor, *Tramway Review;* Alan C Baker; Alan Brotchie; the late John Gillham; Nick Kelly; Colin Laidler; Geoff Lumb; Don Quail; Chris Sims; Roger A Smith for his modern rendering of very old and tatty maps; and, David Voice.

CONTENTS

The Edinburgh Street Tramways Co was one of the earliest horse tramways in the country, opening on 6 November 1871. Operating almost 19 miles of standard gauge route, the last horse cars operated in Leith on 2 November 1906 and Edinburgh on 24 August 1907. *Gerald Hartley*

The Southampton Tramways Co operated a standard gauge horse tramway in the town from 5 May 1879 until 1 July 1898 when it was taken over by the Corporation. The last horse trams operated on 2 August 1901. *Gerald Hartley*

With its first route opened on 6 October 1873, the standard gauge Sheffield Tramways Co operated horse trams over a network of 9½ route miles. Taken over by the Corporation on 11 July 1896, the last horse trams operated on 11 November 1902. *Gerald Hartley*

Introduction

The genesis of this book lay in a series of talks given sometime ago but subsequently updated as more information and illustrations became available. As we are covering the period up to the beginning of electric tram services, for practical purposes we may take this as around 1900. In effect then we are going to look at (mainly) urban mass road transport for a period of 30 years from the passing of the 1870 Tramways Act. Technically horse trams were simple and familiar to Victorians in as much as the horse was the mainstay of road transport whereas the steam tram was always regarded with suspicion. To some extent I can almost understand this among the working classes as, until later, there were only two holidays allowed — May Day and Christmas Day or Boxing Day (the latter being common as servants were required to work Christmas Day so they were granted the following days to take a box of left-over food or whatever to their relatives) — and so urban transport, or the necessity for it, hardly entered their lives. Walking to and from work for the mill or factory hand was the norm, although eventually even the steam tram was to give both men and women flexibility of employment.

Horse trams were very expensive to operate and logically fares were very high — it's interesting to note that, in real terms the cost per mile was far greater than today's buses — and so were the province of the middle class. Now this was a group of people who used railway trains and understood and admired the advances in shipping, communication and all forms of technology. So, to some extent, they were probably inclined to accept the possibility of steam trams, albeit with a strong sense of nimbyism. As long as the trams went via Shuttlecock Road, which comprised mainly the backs of factories with no passenger traffic on offer, then they would happily allow the work to proceed but if Badminton Road, with all its houses, was chosen, then all the usual claims of smoke, dirt, noise and steam would be raised. The upper classes were little affected although many of them were shareholders and tended to be 'nominal' directors.

Towards the very end of the period we also find a number of other railed road transport methods appearing, including cable cars, which will be covered in the companion volume on battery/accumulator, fireless and compressed air. None of these had a long-term impact. Two of the most interesting aspects of the whole story are the advances in rail design and metallurgical quality control. However, for reasons that I have never really understood, there seems to have been little exchange of information between heavy rail engineers and their light rail confrères

A curious hand-tinted postcard sent on 18 February 1909 from Kensington, London. The curiosity lies in the fact that, although Douglas No 30 was built as a toastrack horse tram by George F Milnes at Birkenhead in 1894, the printer has tried to modernise the car by scrubbing out the horse and substituting a trolley-pole for use under the (non-existent) overhead. David Voice, the Tramway & Light Railway Society's archivist, suggests this was the result of an ill-fated attempt by the operator to electrify the line in 1897. Before this could be acted upon, the largest bank on the Isle of Man, Dumbell's, failed and the company — the Isle of Man Tramways & Electric Power Co — became bankrupt. The Corporation took over the 3ft 0in gauge line in 1902 and this fake was probably printed in 1906 when electric cars again became a possibility. No 30 was withdrawn in 1950 and broken up two years later.

— quite illogical when one considers the research teams that worked not only for the big rail companies but also the manufacturers and the rolling mills.

Within the text are just three maps, but each shows a different aspect of the subject. Worcester (page 20) had a typical small horse-drawn layout totalling 3¼ miles, which never grew despite various plans and was superseded by electric trams. Leicester (page 12) was far larger in mileage — 8½ — and was rather better off in both double track and passing loops, both of which would allow for a more intense service. Birmingham (page 44), as befitted a then-growing city had, by 1899, the greatest variety of working, including horse-drawn, steam, cable, and battery/accumulator trams plus horse buses. Although the cut-off date is nominally 1900, I have included the final runs of the orthodox steam trams that continued to operate into the 20th century.

Horse Trams

It is traditional to commence a book with the phrase 'in the beginning'. The problem here is that the beginning of tramways or tramroads is shrouded in mystery. The Romans, naturally, devised a scheme that remained in use for a thousand years or more, that of laying parallel tracks of marble through streets thus enabling carts to have a reasonably smooth road. In the Harz mountains, in Germany, some genius dreamed up the idea of using baulks of timber in a similar manner, in this case to allow for the transport of both timber and coal. Obviously this idea spread and in 1603-04, Huntingdon Beaumont is credited with building the first documented tramway in Britain. When his lease for the land used by the two miles of the Wollaton Wagonway in the East Midlands was renewed in 1604 it included the salient phrase whereby he was allowed to carry coals 'alonge the passage now laid with rails'. What we do not know is whether this line had wooden rails and, if so, whether these were capped by iron strips and indeed whether or not the wheels had flanges.

The Somersetshire Tramways Co Ltd was sometimes known as the Somerton, Keinton Mandeville & Castle Cary Tramways [Syndicate] Ltd, which at least will give a clue where this tramway — a vestige of a hopelessly over-ambitious scheme — ended up trying to go. Subscriptions opened on 7 November and closed on 11 November 1896 for half the permitted capital — ie £30,000 — the agreement being to pay £1 on application, £1 on allotment of the shares and the balance in calls of £1 at intervals of not less than two months. For your money you got one or more shares in the line of 'about' 14 miles, the first section of 'between 6 and 7 miles, is half-ballasted, the sleepers are on the ground, also the larger portion of the rails delivered and the remainder on order'. This tramway at one time spoke of the traffics accruing from Kingweston (population 125), Lydford (122 and Alford (111) — presumably it hoped no-one knew how tiny these villages were. Some part of the tramway — Keinton to Castle Cary — opened for freight, albeit horse-drawn in late 1896/early 1897, but the Great Western Railway had plans of its own and bought out the company lock, stock and barrel to the degree that in March 1899 it was said that 'the Keinton Tramway has been finally abandoned'; the GWR opened its 'cut-off' route from Castle Cary to Langport on 21 July 1906. This Form of Application is a true rarity and self-explanatory.

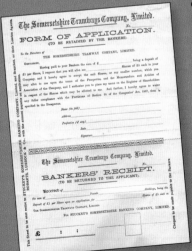

Horse tram No 12 heads along Benson Street, Linthorpe; this line was a relic of an 1875 scheme put forward by the Middlesbrough & Stockton Tramways Co, although, when seen here, the whole operation belonged to the Imperial Tramways Co, which had plans to extend the network of lines in the Tees-side area, many of which were never built; unusually the local councils required the right to purchase the tramways every seven years rather than the 21 permitted under the 1870s Tramways Act.

A commercial postcard sent from Morecambe on 14 September 1892 to a recipient in Huddersfield records a horse tram passing the town's clock tower. At this time the horse trams were operated by the Morecambe Tramways Co, which had introduced them on 3 June 1887. They were to survive until 15 January 1912 when they were replaced by petrol trams that lasted until 24 October 1924. Morecambe Corporation also operated horse trams, from 26 July 1912 until 6 October 1926.

Clock Tower and Promenade, Morecambe.

North Metropolitan tram No 217 was supplied in 1879 by John Stephenson (1809-1893), an Irishman who had emigrated to New York and set up his works there on West 27th Street. Despite bankruptcy following bank failures, Stephenson recovered to become one of the most important tramcar suppliers of the late 19th century. The knifeboard seating on the upper deck of No 217 was later replaced by transverse seats. The driver and conductor were paid between 4s 6d and 6s 0d according to seniority for an 11½-hour working day, with the trams operating normally between 7am and 10.30pm. As a snap shot, by 1891 the North Met had 376 tramcars, 12 horse buses and 103 miscellaneous vehicles. Each pair of horses was not allowed to work more than 16 miles per days; put to work at the age of five, each horse only had a working life of four years and in 1891 3,587 horses were at work of which 200 were sick. In the six months to December 1891 315 horses died and 95 sold as useless — that was the price paid for horse tram services.

Little improvement on this pattern of wooden tramway was made in England, although the Bebside Railway in Northumberland, carrying coals from the Cowpen, Benside and Bedlington areas to the River Blythe and opened in 1608, was the first line to be credited with using 'sacrificial' wooden rails on top of the main baulks. It appears certain that strips of iron were placed on top of the underlying oak or fir 'rails' in Whitehaven about 1738 but, initially at least, the cost of iron ensured the continued use of wood until the early 19th century. A retrograde move seems to have been the change from resilient wooden sleepers to stone blocks, although from this came a 'dead end' method of fastening, involving each metre length rail having a hole at one end through which an iron nail was driven into the wooden plug filling a hole in the stone block. During a survey carried out into miles of these tramroads in the 1970s, it seemed the gauge was maintained solely by the stone

Huddersfield Corporation decided to opt to lay its own track and then lease the route to a suitable contractor as was permitted by 1870's Tramways Act. The terms of the Act meant that the Corporation could not just sit on its hands and refuse all offers but, when no-one came forward that would ensure a reasonable return on the ratepayers' investment, the Corporation was eventually permitted to operate the route itself. Horse trams were operated for a brief period between 1885 and 1888, when this photograph of No 7 was taken. Steam trams operated in the town from 1883 to 1902 and electric cars from 1901 to 1940; the latter were largely replaced by trolleybuses from 1933 onwards.

blocks. Around 1797, in the north-east, we find compound rails capable of being used by both flanged and flangeless wheels but still an iron tramroad cost about £1,000 per mile against half that for a wooden way.

The first true 'real' railway was the Surrey Iron Railway, which used a plate rail of 'L' section and ran from the River Thames at Wandsworth Creek to Croydon; this freight line was fine when it ran alongside the local, mostly unmade, roads and was some 8½ miles (13.68km) in length with a 1½-mile (2.4km) branch. It is said that, as well as horses, mules and donkeys were used from its opening on 24 July 1803. Toll rates 'for all goods … whatsoever' carried into the dock at Wandsworth were 4d per ton but elsewhere 3d per ton sufficed. 'Fractions of a Quarter of a Ton to be considered as a Quarter, but all fractions of a Mile as a Mile.' However, this tramway lost money, not least from covering claims for broken wheels when they met the upstand of the 'L'-shaped rails.

A man who might well have been our hero was George Francis Train, who engineered and opened his first horse tramway from Birkenhead along Conway Street to Birkenhead Park; this was a distance of about 1½ miles and the line opened on 30 August 1860, but alas our hero had a problem. He used step rail, which, even in a

Two views of horse trams in Leicester. The first (above left) is clearly carefully posed and is a well-known view of No 9 at the Groby Road terminus. The second shows a more brutal 'drag' climbing towards Humberstone Gate in the 1890s. Although steam trams were tried under the aegis of Henry Hughes in 1876, it was perhaps too early (despite the proximity of his Loughborough works) as the burghers of Leicester turned their collective faces against steam and the Leicester Tramways Co had, perforce, to retain horse operation. The company's last annual return, dated 31 December 1900, showed it had 87 tramcars (78 two-horse and nine one-horse), 86 buses and seven brakes (open air for parties), which required a stud of 355 horses. A total of 835,000 miles were run in that year and nearly 10 million passenger trips were made, with revenue of £43,192 and a dividend to shareholders of 5%. The company does seem to have looked after its horses, with maize, oats, beans, bran, hay and clover being purchased along with sawdust, moss litter and 'sundries'. The cost of horses was meticulously recorded: January to June 1900 each cost 11s ⅓d but this rose to 11s 5¾d in the second half of the year reflecting the general rise in prices. After takeover by the Corporation, electrification followed in 1904.

modified form, projected ⅝th in (16mm) above the road surface, causing enough damage that two years later this trackwork was ripped up and replaced by grooved rail on the French Loubat pattern; in Paris these were laid on longitudinal timbers carried upon transverse wooden sleepers, the latter acting in place of the tie rods (which were invented later). What really makes no sense is that Loubat's grooved rail was in use in Paris in 1857, whereas Train persisted in his use of step rails in laying his three London lines — Marble Arch to Notting Hill via Bayswater Road, Westminster Abbey to Pimlico (now Victoria) railway station and from the south side of Westminster Bridge to Kennington Gate — any or all of which could and should have been profitable. After all, Train's horse trams were very commodious, measuring 23ft (7.32m) in length and 7ft 0in (2.13m) in width, with excellent ventilation, especially in contrast to the fetid atmosphere of the cramped horse buses. Although only using two horses per tram, the Parisian horse cars were said to be capable of 18mph even when carrying their maximum capacity of 60 passengers plus 10 standing on the open platform. Train claimed 8mph (12.87km/h) for 70 passengers.

When the proprietors of the Lincoln Tramways Co began their planning in 1880, they were full of ideas and dreams, but eventually their one and only route — from Bracebridge to Cornhill — was opened on 8 September 1882. The 20min run cost 2d in 1d fare stages. Most cars, like the one illustrated, sat around 20 passengers, although the introduction of workmen's half-penny fares in 1901 proved successful enough to require the fleet to be augmented. The presence of two busy railway level crossings in the city made time-keeping difficult, but in the year 1899/1900 the 1¾-mile route generated an income of £3,162 with expenses of £2,302 that included £734 on the horses and £123 on animal renewals. A total of 70,714 miles were run by the nine trams and 21 horses with 607,374 passenger journeys. Shareholders received a net profit of £859.

The Marble Arch line opened in March 1861, with the other two lines following later the same year. However, the evidence is overwhelming that, if a dog-cart, carriage or cab was driven across these rails at even a reasonable speed, a wheel could easily be wrenched off its axle and even the heavy wheels of omnibuses began to collapse, upsetting the vehicle and passengers alike as the dagger-like shards of glass flew among them. Moreover, there was an outcry from what we would today call 'animal conservationists', inasmuch as horses and ponies were having their hooves damaged, with many becoming fit only for cats'-meat. After the rails were ripped up at the end of 1862 it was to be eight years before horse trams again ran in London.

In the Potteries the third successful tramway using step rails opened in 1863 but two years later orthodox grooved rail was introduced.

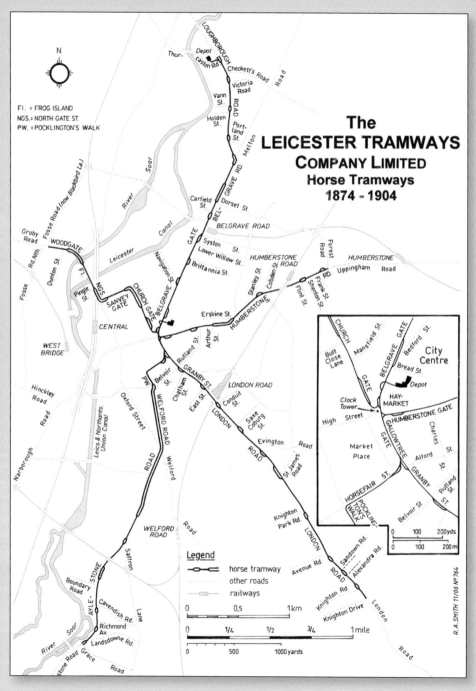

The
LEICESTER TRAMWAYS
COMPANY LIMITED
Horse Tramways
1874 - 1904

FI. = FROG ISLAND
NGS.= NORTH GATE ST.
PW. = POCKLINGTON'S WALK

In 1892/93 the primary operator in Birmingham — Birmingham Central Tramways (as the predecessor of City of Birmingham Tramways shown here) — published the relative costs of the forms of haulage power it used and produced quite complex tables to the profit each generated: steam 4.777d/mile run; horse 0.81d; cable 6.37d; and, electricity (battery) a loss of 0.17d/mile run. Another comparison is of great interest: the steam cars ran 1,226,000 miles, horse 648,000, cable 641,000 but electricity only 141,000. Much of the horse traffic was on the Nechells route — as shown here — where 10 special narrow horse trams were in use. The route was electrified in 1906 and was later the pioneering tram to trolleybus conversion.

In 1870, the Tramways Act outlawed step rails and grooved rails took over — but the styles of rails available showed by their variety how disparate the whole industry really was. Horse trams turned up in almost every town and city that was forward looking with some 140 corporations and companies involved although their service lives varied enormously. For example, the Aldershot & Farnborough Light Railway Co arrived in 1881 but disappeared two years later although the two cars later trundled up and down the 2½ miles of route again between 1888 and 1898. Conversely, Nottingham Corporation ended up with 10½ miles of trackwork with 38 cars running from 1898 to 1901, the system having been bought lock, stock and barrel from the Nottingham & District Tramways Co Ltd in 1897, the company having operated the cars since 1878. One of the earliest and most successful in terms of mileage was the London Street Tramways, which commenced operation in 1871 and, at its peak, had 136 cars running an intensive service over a 13½-mile network.

Obviously the photographic captions give more detail on individual companies. But other examples include the Exeter Tramways Co Ltd, which had three very short routes totalling a mere 2½ miles, which were in use from April 1882 until April 1905, although the Corporation electrified and extended the routes then. The electric trams were to survive until April 1931. The first horse cars in Exeter were tiny little vehicles: 3ft 6in gauge, single-deckers seating 16 plus four standing. These were hardly viable with four horses required plus two platform staff; in all eight of these small cars, painted a bright yellow with chocolate lettering, entered service, followed by six double-deck trams in the mid-1890s; for some reason, by the time of the Corporation purchase, only four double-deckers and one of the single-deck cars remained in service. One interesting note relates to the horses used; unlike the majority of companies which purchased their horses on the open market, Exeter had a deal with a local farmer who trained the horses using carts, then passing them on for a stint on the trams, buying them back after an average of three years. However, references to convictions of the tram drivers for cruelty to horses was reported to the authorities by a local animal welfare body appear in local papers with some regularity — a fact that marred the company's reputation.

The 1870 Tramways Act — in full 'An Act to facilitate the construction and to regulate the working of Tramways' — had one interesting limitation inasmuch as it did not apply to Ireland (then all one country and still part of the United Kingdom) and most Irish tramways were to be built on an entirely different basis. One definition that we need to remember is that 'The term "road" shall mean any carriageway being a public highway'. Not only did the tramway companies have to maintain the roadway between the rails but also 18in (457mm)on each side — a total, for single track, standard-gauge line, of 7ft 8½in (2.35m) and 6ft 6in (1.98m) for a single 3ft 6in narrow-gauge track. Moreover, this onerous provision did not give the promoters *carte blanche* to proceed; typically, out of 266 miles proposed in the London area in 1870, only 61 were authorised.

The poor spavined horse in the first of these two photographs was clearly towards the end of its days when photographed around the start of the 20th century. Four miles long, the Pwllheli & Llanbedrog Tramway opened on 1 August 1896 and was owned and operated by Solomon Andrews, a Cardiff entrepreneur. The line was designed to encourage visitors to Tremedoc Bay, which Andrews hoped to develop into another Rhyl or similar resort. According to the late Roger Kidner, who provided both of the photographs, the horse was quite typical of Andrews's animals in the early days; however, pressure from the council and from irate ladies writing to newspapers led to improvements as evinced by the fact that the little Welsh cob trotting along Cardiff Road looks quite plump! The tramway closed in 1927.

One good aspect was of the Act lay in the banning of any but grooved rails, and another was that the lines were to be inspected and passed by Board of Trade officials before the track could be opened for passenger service. The shortage of men versed in tramway work was all too apparent in those early days and the majority of lines failed their first inspections (which were very thorough indeed) or received advisory notices for relatively minor items — 'This line maybe opened for the carriage of passengers subject to the completion of the following works ... .' The engineer would hustle the contractors and the contractors, probably very unwillingly, would do as skimpy a job as they could, while being undercapitalised and in need of the final payment to start work on another line.

Another problem inherent in the 1870 Act was that the relevant local authorities must approve the methods used to construct tramways in their areas, and were given the powers to purchase all the lines, fittings, etc 21 years after their Act was obtained and every seventh year thereafter. When, after 1878-80, it became very evident that horse-drawn tramways were not a gold mine, investment in new lines and extensions to the first tranche declined to a trickle.

At this point a few statistics will give a good idea of the problems inherent in a horse tramway. The tramway featured is the North Metropolitan Tramways Co, the largest system in the UK at the time — some 59 miles (79km) in length. Opened on 9 May 1870, its early horses were hired from the London General Omnibus Co, but from June 1878 the company made a decision to have its own stables. After purchasing the lines of the North London Tramways, the company's rolling stock looked this this at 31 December 1891:

Fully equipped street cars to carry 52 passengers each	35
Fully equipped street cars to carry 50 passengers each	4
Fully equipped street cars to carry 46 passengers each	271
Fully equipped street cars to carry 40 passengers each	62
Fully equipped street cars to carry 20 passengers each	4
Total	**376**
Omnibuses to carry 26 passengers each	12
Carts, traps, vans and trolleys	64
Water-carts	25
Forage vans	10
Brakes	2
Horse Conveyances	2
Total rolling stock	**491**
Horses	**3,587**

The whole expenditure had been £1,412,476 or £31,388 per mile open, the tramcars totalling £66,430 and horses £133,032. The least pleasant statistic relates to the horses which, when bought in at three years old, were life-expired after only five years' work. The following table shows the number of horses at the end of each half-year period to 31 December 1891:

End of half-year	In good condition	Sick	Lame	Total	Died in half-year	Sold in half-year	Total
June 1889	3,027	21	101	3,149	118	123	241
Dec 1889	2,963	58	105	3,126	176	115	291
June 1890	3,239	24	83	3,346	156	134	290
Dec 1890	3,147	97	111	3,355	214	109	323
June 1891	3,444	60	86	3,590	243	69	312
Dec 1891	3,386	59	142	3,587	315	95	410
Averages	3,201	53	105	3,359	204	107	311

It shows that of the average total of horses, 95.3% were in good condition and 4.7% disabled.

Each tramcar cost an average of £150 new with around 20 being under repair at any one time out of a fleet of 376 at its peak. Passenger numbers, which were rising steadily, stood at 75 million in 1891, each paying an average of 2.64d. The cars ran 7.5 million miles, (12.07 million km) and receipts totalled £430,828. The next table shows more clearly than words just why horse tramways struggled to be viable in a word — the horse:

Item	1888	1889	1891	1891 proportional parts of total expenditure	1891 expenditure per mile run
Direct expenditure	£	£	£	Per cent	Pence
Horses	130,226	137,250	160,244	46.34	4.85
Wages of drivers and pole shifters	31,374	34,780	38,004	12.56	1.21
Repair of cars	10,732	10,114	10,545	3.55	0.33
Maintenance of way	25,172	29,369	25,090	8.50	0.80
Traffic charges	49,239	53,861	60,046	17.95	1.91
General charges	9.021	9,440	11,367	3.59	0.36
Rent	2,916	3,111	2,852	0.84	0.09
Direct	258,680	277,925	308,148	93.33	9.55

It has never been entirely clear to the author why steam trams of the Sunderland Tramways Co failed. The locomotives had been built by R & W Hawthorn to an already successful design of the Swiss Locomotive & Engine Works, Winterthur and, fitted with a 'pistol' type boiler, seem to have been a neat and workmanlike product. However, fail they did and reversion to horse-drawn trams became the order of the day. The lines had first opened on 28 April 1879, albeit just over 3½ miles of the planned 7¼, and, on 31 July, the first through journey on the combined Christ Church-Roker and Monkwearmouth-Gray Road routes took place. For those (if any) who paid, the fare was 2d.

In all, with taxes, insurance, etc, the company's total expenditure for 1891 was £330,814 against receipts of £430,828, leaving at the very most £100,000 to pay dividends on £1.4 million capital expended. The reasons given by the engineer have an uncommonly familiar ring about them: 'The high rate of expenditure in 1891 was due to the rise in the price of forage, increase of wages and unfavourable weather.' The horses' diet was reasonable — one London firm gave its animals 20% sawdust — and included maize, oats, beans, bran, peas and hay with straw and moss litter for bedding.

The company was relatively successful, eventually selling out to the nascent London Transport; by contrast Hull, opened in July 1873 on flat routes that were, however, bedevilled by numerous railway crossings, only survived until 1887, when the company — Hull Street Tramways Co — was forced into liquidation. The company's 39 cars were presumably dispersed although the nine route miles (14.5km) remained until Hull Corporation purchased the remnants on 1 August 1895 for electrification.

Initially opened from Stirling to Bridge of Allan on 27 July 1874, the Bridge of Allan, Stirling & St Ninians Tramway was extended to St Ninians in January 1898. The line closed on 20 May 1920 as a result of competition from buses. The tram seen here was built by the Tramways Cars & Works Co of Glasgow and is a neat design rarely seen elsewhere. Eventually the basic fleet was augmented by the acquisition of a second-hand tram from Edinburgh; this was adapted to be self-propelled through a petrol engine in part due to a shortage of horses during World War 1. Bridge of Allan was a spa town, with a high tourist flow, but today is more reliant upon university life.

A favourite for many years was the Fairbourne Tramway in North Wales, which followed a circuitous route — north, south, west and then north again — to Penrhyn Point where it met the Barmouth ferry. Originally a line serving a brickworks that opened in 1890, it then carried passengers in two toastrack cars. Closed to horse traction in 1916 — the last two animals being 'called up' for war service — the line is now the very narrow gauge (12¼in/311mm) Fairbourne Steam Railway that runs two miles (3.2km) between the village of Fairbourne and Porth Penrhyn.

The two university towns, Oxford and Cambridge, dealt with any chance of modernisation by violent — indeed vitriolic — attacks on 'unsightly overhead wires'. Opened on 28 January 1882, Oxford's horse tramway ceased to operate on 31 December 1913, whilst Cambridge's operated from 28 October 1880 to 18 February 1914, both being replaced by nice smelly, smoky petrol-engined buses.

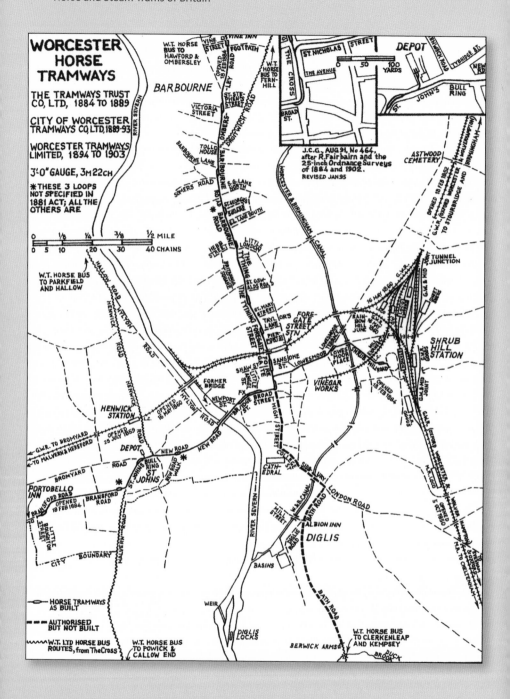

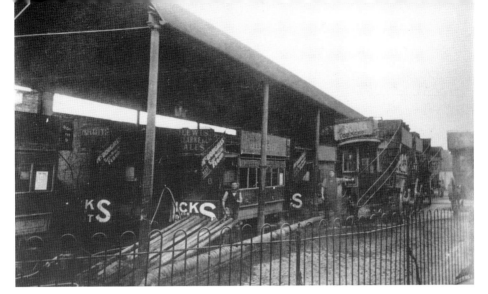

There is some doubt as to exactly when this photograph of horse trams in Worcester was taken; dates from 1899 to 1904 have been quoted but the evidence would tend to suggest that a later date is more likely as the horse buses — which the tram operator also ran to act as feeder services without the cost of laying track — appear to be in poor condition, something that occurred with the arrival of electric trams in the city.

Ryde Pier is actually three separate piers in one and was the home to a good number of unusual tramway operations; steam was tried in the early days (1881-84) but the vibration loosened the fastenings. A 0.39-mile long standard-gauge horse tramway was used from 29 August 1864 to shift the passengers to and from the steamers as well as others who simply wanted to make the trip. The line was extended to a junction with the railway at St John's Road station, making the run 1.12 miles from 7 August 1871; it was, however, later cut back. Electric services started on 13 March 1886 and later still petrol trams serviced the line. The walkway on the right is still open; the centre tramway is now semi-derelict but the line on the left, with the horse trams, is now operated by an electric train.

Preserved Chesterfield & Brampton horse car No 8. Known by the Board of Trade as the Chesterfield, Brampton & Whittington, the company's permitted capital to fund the line's construction was £30,000 although only £9,650 was raised. In 1883 a note records that the present directors had only worked the line for two months; prior to this it had been leased. The new company — Chesterfield & District Tramways Co Ltd — ran the line until 1897 when it passed to the corporation for a mere £2,050. Plans for the extension from Brampton to Whittington along with the development of a couple of steam tram routes were abandoned. In 1883, the line made a profit of £24 from three trams operated by a dozen horses; in 1885, however, a net loss of £26 was recorded with income of £877 and expenditure of £903 from the 1½-mile long route. A total of 123,526 passengers had been carried with average receipts of 0.62d per passenger! By 1891, the route had shrink to 1¼ miles but a profit of £68 resulted from income of £762 although average fare per passenger had declined to 0.42d.

In Ireland, the Cork Tramways Co Ltd opened its first route on 12 September 1872. The tramway's purpose was to connect the town's four railway termini with each other and to serve the city centre but, alas, by December 1875 it was gone. In due course, in February 1898, a new company opened an electric tramway; in the intervening years, taxis served well enough.

What makes the first tramway in Cork so important is that, during its brief life, the trams were known as 'Train cars'; this may have been a reference to their serving the railway lines but the route used was one that had been surveyed by George Francis Train way back in 1860. And, if that was not enough, the first manager was no less than James Clifton Robinson, 'the Tramway King', who ended up as managing director of Bristol Tramways, a large group, the Imperial Tramways Co, London United Tramways and the Corris Railway. Born in 1848, he was first employed by Train, who he then surpassed as both a visionary and practical engineer. He died from a heart attack while on tour in New York on 6 November 1910, but never forgot Cork, marrying a girl from the town, who, it was said, he had met on a tram!

Although there were flirtations with steam trams in Sheffield, the hills defeated them. As a result of the provisions within the Tramways Act, Sheffield Corporation was unable to operate tramcars itself although it could purchase land, lay track, etc and then lease this to any private operator prepared too pay interest on loans raised to pay the cost of the trackwork plus and annual rent (in the case of Sheffield £100 per mile). A particularly nasty clause in the act required the operator to maintain the track and 18in each side of the rails; this was always going to be a bone of contention. The Lady's Bridge-Attercliffe 'Golden Ball' route was the first to be opened, on 6 October 1873, and was served by 12 two-horse and eight one-horse trams supplied by Starbuck Car & Wagon Co of Birkenhead. No 15, seen here at Crich on 22 October 1961, is the sole survivor of this delivery. The author received a copy of the photograph as he was one of the group struggling to rerail the tram using the clearly visible home-made rerailing ramps. The tram behind is Leeds No 446; this was new to Hull in 1909 as No 132 and sold to Leeds in 1942. Based at Crich between 1960 and 1963, the car is now on permanent loan to Hull's Streetlife Museum where it is displayed with Portstewart Kitson engine No 1. *R B Parr*

Called by an Irish writer 'The Stray Tramway', the line to Fintona was opened as a 'proper' railway by the Londonderry & Enniskillen Railway in 1853, but, as the company's route was extended to Dromore Road, the L&ER started its extension ¾-mile up the road at Fintona Junction, leaving the town on a branch from 16 January 1854. Freight services remained steam hauled but, in due course, the passenger service became horse drawn for economy and remained so until closure on 1 October 1957. Four-wheel tram No 381 (now preserved), the second horse tram, was ordered from the Metropolitan Carriage & Wagon Co and delivered in 1883 (the year in which the L&ER was absorbed into the Great Northern Railway [Ireland]) and was a rarity inasmuch as all three classes of travel were offered when new: first and second in the saloon and third on top.

Opposite top: York was a near miss for steam trams but the horses of the York Tramways Co operated from October 1880 to 1886 when they were replaced by those of a new company — the City of York Tramways Co. As a result of the climb up to Micklegate, a trace horse was essential to assist the tram up the ascent. The smartly uniformed driver may be an indication that the photograph was taken after the Corporation takeover in 1909.

Opposite bottom: Worcester New Road includes a steep climb up to St John's Bull Ring and a trace horse was also essential to assist a vehicle up the gradient. In the reverse direction, the trace horse was quite happy to trot alongside the tram unaccompanied by the normally attendant boy.

The Steam Tram:
Building, Running and Accidents

If the wrong pattern of trackwork was selected it could prove to be the Achilles' heel of any tramway; in early days, engineers seemed to a large extent to work in isolation and to regard their tramway as separate from other road users. All too often the track bed was laid for a load of, say, a maximum of five tons — a fully laden horse tram — and seemingly no account was taken of other traffic, especially the heavy drays in use for metal castings or piled high with cotton or wool bales, requiring eight or more horses to drag them. There was nothing worse than the pounding the wagons' iron wheels gave the track as they lurched and twisted through the mill or factory gates.

For some time there was a desire by engineers to use wood somewhere in the track base, mainly to give some degree of resilience but also to deaden the perceived sound and vibration (despite the fact that adjacent could be a forge-master's shop with drop hammers working all day), which might just have worked if the specification had been adhered to. This normally called for the use of imported and expensive timber like Keruing, Iroko or Jarrah, but the contractor, under pressure, would often substitute a softer native timber. Hearing the cost of Jarrah, one pompous local council member asked the engineer what was wrong 'with good English oak'. The engineer tried to explain, but a few weeks later found oak in use by the engineer; it seemed that the wood came from the timber yard owned by the councillor. After a few bitter words, the engineer resigned as the thought of relaying 400yd of track could not be entertained.

Looking at any road, for drainage purposes the camber of the surface falls towards the gutter, so that the fully laden trailer with perhaps 70 people on board — at least eight tons in all — is trying to slide down to its low side and unlike motor-cars no compensation was possible for this tendency, and it was reported time and time again how far the bogie tyres on this nearside were worn. The engine meanwhile has the same tendency of lateral movement plus the twisting effect on the frames, motion, and boiler alike, all of which initially wore out the wheels' bearings and axles at a phenomenal rate compared with 'proper' railways, and also undermined even the conservative figures for rolling resistance given in *The Engineer*. Sooner or later, and sadly in many cases it was sooner, the rails would go out of gauge and this oscillation would increase to a point where adjacent to a worn fish-plate, which was no longer capable of holding the rails

The line from Rawtenstall to Burnley was planned as a 3ft 6in line in the early days of steam tramway but was only partially completed, to a different gauge (4ft 0in) and by a new company (the Rossendale Valley Co). After some delays, the company made it as far as Crawshaybooth, opening this section on 12 September 1891 with a half-hourly service from Rawtenstall railway station to the town. Plans for the rest of the line were formally abandoned the following year. This view was one of a sequence recording the construction of the tramway along Burnley Road in June 1891 under the guidance of William Love — seen standing in the centre. He was later to die, on 10 January 1896, in odd circumstances when he 'fell' from a tramcar at Waterfoot, the verdict being accidental death. The final steam trams operated in the Rossendale Valley on 23 July 1909.

together with the result that lumps of the rail flange, invariably on the nearside rail, would sheer off; this being recorded in council minutes with the offending lump of rail being banged down on the council table or perhaps in a more conciliatory mood, handed in at the tramways office.

DICK, KERR & CO.,

ENGINEERS AND CONTRACTORS,

101, LEADENHALL STREET, LONDON, E.C.,

HORSE, STEAM & CABLE TRAMWAY CONTRACTORS,

MANUFACTURERS OF

STEEL GIRDER TRAMWAY RAILS,

Of all Sections from 35 lbs. to 100 lbs. per yard.

Tramway Engines, Winding Engines for Cable Tramways, Pulleys, Ropes, Cars, &c.

ESTIMATES GIVEN FOR LAYING AND EQUIPPING TRAMWAYS, OR LIGHT RAILWAYS OF ANY DESCRIPTION.

ADVERTISEMENTS.

ix

Above: Advert for Dick, Kerr & Co promoting its production of track for horse, steam and cable — but not electric — tramways.

The basis of good trackwork but, after a decade of use, the underlying 12in thick layer of concrete has failed.

To some extent this could be blamed on poor quality control at the rolling mills, metal quality varying enormously, and worse on the short runs required for some 'fancy' trackwork it does seem as though the basic iron was allowed to cool too far in the rolls, the resultant chattering making these lengths crystalline. There were always clauses in contracts allowing for up to 10% wastage, but it is a simple fact that, working with frozen fingers at a very poorly lit excavation in pouring rail, who was going to bother to sort out with a gauge one rail among dozens — human nature being what it is you just get on and use what comes to hand. Tales abound of very strange rail sections (the 'pet' of some patentee friend of the engineer) having to have the groove ground in them by a foot-operated machine — no electricity of course — and others where a luckless apprentice had to drill the holes in iron rails to match the fishplate holes ... his peccadilloes or at least the connivance of everyone to get the job done becoming apparent in a year or two when it was

Track in Halifax is ready for relaying but note the condition of the adjacent track where each tram would work on this weakness. *A E Dixon Collection*

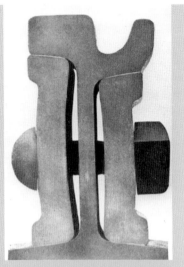

A cross-section demonstrating ideal track design of *circa* 1900.

An advert for a Leeds-based track manufacturer demonstrating some of the various types of track available.

found short bolts had been fitted in the drilled fishplate to appear as though the whole was bolted together ... we do not have space here to show the really mad designs of rails that were tried, but too many followed the chimera of accepting that the rails would wear and throw-away top sections as in our older wood+iron-strip composite rails was the answer. Alas, as with some railway lines where this was tried, the hammer blow from the thrust of the cylinders and unbalanced wheels of the locomotive engines not only affected the 'sacrificial' rail but the carrier rails underneath. And because of the time lapse — perhaps getting on for a decade — the specialised rolls in the works and in one known case the drawings had disappeared. Ultimately variations on the 'Gowan' girder rail were to prove the most satisfactory, but unlike most of the fancy patterns when this rail needed renewal there was no option but to rip up the road, sometimes even including the base concrete which, poor enough quality in the first place, will probably have perished from the road muck — including gallons of horse urine — dripping through from above.

Probably the worst difficulty that the engineer had to face was that of bending the rails to suit the curvature of the road; many of the stranger sections were impossible to shape outside of the mill and wastage was high as estimates were often inaccurate, many rails arriving poorly forged or rolled, so much so that seems to have been accepted practice to allow 10-15% extra for this — which has to be added to the costs, as did the labour of one or two men sawing off the faulty ends of rails. In order to lay track and obtain suitable curvature, specialist equipment — such as track benders — was developed.

Initially the Board of trade was seemingly not too bothered about lifeguards, presumably on the basis that the inherent danger within horse trams lay in the horses and not the actual tram. However, a form of guard did emerge, but those that the author has seen were far from sophisticated and seemed to rely upon the vigilance of the driver — certainly, like all horse-drawn vehicles, the brakes were not much use and one of the complaints levied against steam trams was their ability (certainly with the horizontal boilered cars) to stop very quickly. The big danger, if a child or dog got under the wheels, was that the flanges, running in grooves, would act like bacon slicers. The guards on steam tractors could never be entirely efficient, as the locomotives bounced badly and tended to sit up at the front under the weight of the trailer. Eventually a rather effective brush, which could be easily unhitched by the driver and dropped to the level of the rails, was developed. Prior to this a number of elaborate and probably impossible to maintain 'gadgets' were developed and patented. A Mr Hughes dreamed up this deflector/wire basket/brush in 1894 (Patent No 3015 of 1895).

In the early days of steam trams the vertical Field tube boiler seemed to have many advantages. They were relatively light, compact and, using a geared final drive, appeared really suited for tramway work. Unfortunately build quality seems to have been variable with, axiomatically, the dearest in price as manufactured by Beyer Peacock being by far the better machines.

However, the design had two great failings. The first was that the vertical tubes were prone to scaling in hard water districts; this scale gradually formed what the BoT inspectors regularly called 'an accretion' within the tube, which formed a dead spot when exposed to the furnace heat until eventually the wastage of the metal

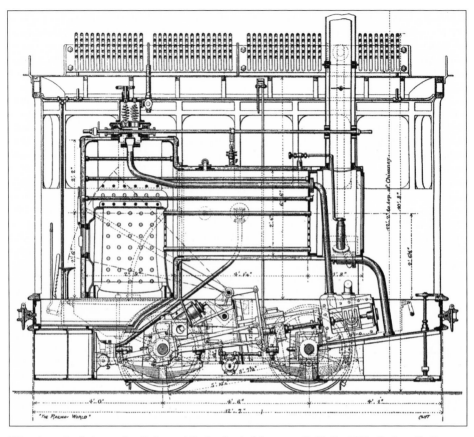

This cutaway is of a locomotive that was at the forefront of those supplied in the 1880s. Designed by Norman Scott Russell for the Falcon Engine & Car Works of Loughborough, these machines were a far cry from those built by his predecessor Henry Hughes. The design is an amazing example of compression.

and the lack of water caused an explosion. Secondly, it was very hard indeed for anyone properly to inspect these tubes in a hot boiler with only candlelight available at, for example, 2am on a winter's morning.

When these boilers exploded, steam and boiling water roared out at 140psi, more often that not seriously scalding the driver who (unless he subscribed to the hospital fund) would be taken home to live or die. And these men's conditions could be awful; as late as 1897 a driver living at 13 Rose Street, Coseley had one room, 10ft by 12ft, in which he lived with a 40-year-old backward daughter, a 16-year-old son, a 14-year-old daughter plus five other children as well as (temporarily) a 22-year-old son with wife. No wonder the driver died from secondary infection.

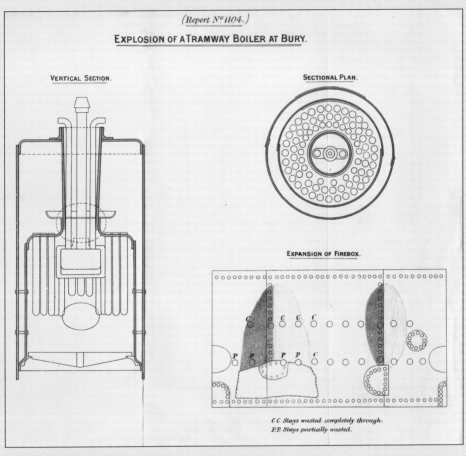

(Report Nº 1104.)

EXPLOSION OF A TRAMWAY BOILER AT BURY.

VERTICAL SECTION.

SECTIONAL PLAN.

EXPANSION OF FIREBOX.

C.C Stays wasted completely through.
P.P. Stays partially wasted.

The drawing shows the design of a Field boiler recorded following an explosion in it at the Bury depot of the Bury, Rochdale & Oldham Tramways Co on 1 May 1898. The boiler was 16-years-old and 'the firebox was bulged and having lost its cylindrical form and its original supports, it was unable to resist the pressure to which it was subjected, or any pressure at all' according to a contemporary report. The force of the explosion turned the engine up on its end and extinguished all the lights of the depot; William Cooper died of his wounds on the following day.

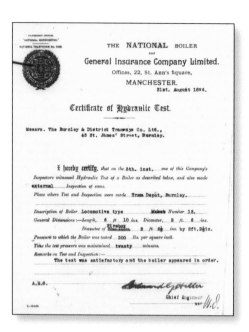

A boiler certificate for Burnley & District No 13; the locomotive was a Falcon engine designed by Norman Scott Russell and delivered in 1885.

A drawing that accompanied the report into the mud-hole failure at Blackburn; the design, in engineering terms, was a complete nonsense as it was impossible to see if the bolt was properly located and, working blind, locating a worn round-headed bolt into an oval hole, was never going to be easy.

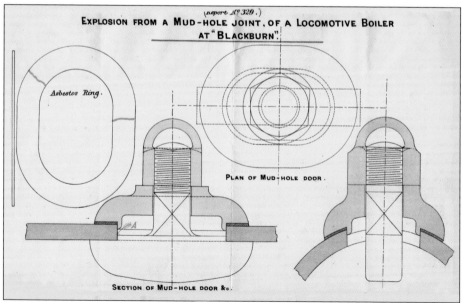

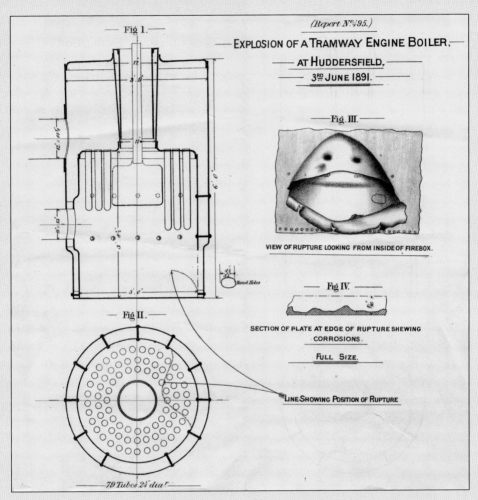

(Report Nº 495.)

— EXPLOSION OF A TRAMWAY ENGINE BOILER, —

—— AT HUDDERSFIELD. ——

—— 3ʳᵈ JUNE 1891. ——

— Fig. 1.—

— Fig. III. —

VIEW OF RUPTURE LOOKING FROM INSIDE OF FIREBOX.

— Fig II. —

— Fig IV. —

SECTION OF PLATE AT EDGE OF RUPTURE SHEWING CORROSIONS.

FULL SIZE.

LINE SHOWING POSITION OF RUPTURE

—— 79 Tubes 2¼ diaʳ ——

A drawing that accompanied the official report into the Crosland Moor accident. In the brutal words of the report: 'The explosion was caused by the fire-box having wasted away to such an extent from corrosion as to be no longer able to withstand the pressure of steam.'

399

THOMAS GREEN & SON,
LIMITED,

Smithfield Iron Works, Leeds
AND
SURREY WORKS,
BLACKFRIARS ROAD, LONDON, S.E.

ENGINEERS AND MANUFACTURERS OF

GREEN'S IMPROVED LOCO-TYPE TRAMWAY ENGINES
With either Inside or Outside Cylinders,
HIGH PRESSURE OR COMPOUND PATTERN.

ALSO TANK LOCOMOTIVES & LIGHT RAILWAY ENGINES
AND VAUX'S PATENT TRAMWAY COUPLINGS.

These Engines may be seen at work on the following Tramway Companies' Lines, viz:—

The Bradford & Shelf,
The Dundee & District,
The Bradford Tram
and Omnibus,
The Blackburn and
Over Darwen,
The Leeds,
The Accrington Cor-
poration,
The Birmingham and
Midland,
The Blackburn Cor-
poration,
The Rossendale Valley,
The Dropool and Mar-
fleet, Hull,
The Wolverton and
Stony Stratford,
St. Helen's,
AND OTHERS.

PATENT LIFT FOR TRAMWAY ENGINES,
TOOLS AND FITTINGS FOR TRAM-ENGINE SHEDS.
OVERHEAD TRAVELLERS, HAND-POWER AND STEAM CRANES.
PATENT STEAM ROAD ROLLERS, TRACTION, STATIONARY, AND VERTICAL ENGINES AND BOILERS COMBINED.
STEAM WINCHES, PUMPS, &c.
Specifications, Price Lists, and References on Application.

An all-purpose engineering company, Thomas Green & Son Ltd of Leeds built anything from locomotives to lawn mowers. Records show that, aside from a handful of unsuccessful vertical boilered tram engines, around 178 locomotive boilered tram 'dummies' were delivered between 1885 and 1906, of which a handful were road rather than rail based. This contemporary advert highlights some of the operators that the company had supplied.

The Accrington Corporation Steam Tramways Co operated steam trams over a nine-mile 4ft 0in-gauge line between 5 April 1886 until into municipal ownership in September 1907. The last steam tram operated in Accrington on 31 December 1907 and Haslingden on 27 September 1908. *Gerald Hartley*

The Bradford & Shelf Tramways Co was one of the three companies that served the city. It operated a network of 7½ miles of 4ft 0in gauge from 8 September 1884 until the Corporation took over on 31 January 1902. The last steam tram operated on 1 April 1903. *Gerald Hartley*

All steam boilers were required to be hydraulically tested, although this did not include an internal inspection, which was the responsibility of the engineer or foreman and the boilersmith. A boiler certificate was a Board of Trade requirement as insurance was compulsory as without this operation became illegal.

The mud-hole door was just that as it enabled the boilersmith or labourer to clean out the sludge within a boiler that was an inevitable consequence of boiling water, particularly in Victorian days when water often came from a well. These were prone to failure; one such accident occurred in Blackburn. According to the contemporary report by the Inspecting Officer (the Engineer Surveyor-in-General of the BoT) 'the asbestos ring jointing the mud-hole to the boiler was completely blown out, and the hot water, &c, was forced through the aperture into the cab of the engine where the driver was standing ... William Mercer, the driver of the engine, was severely scalded on the legs, arms, and neck. He was conveyed to the Blackburn and East Lancashire Hospital shortly after the explosion, and has since died.' The asbestos ring was only nine-months old and the inspector censured the manufacturer, Thos Green & Co, for its design. The manager of the operator, Blackburn Corporation Tramways Co, had had plans, sadly unfulfilled, to modify the fitting.

There was, inevitably, a human price to be paid for the failure of steam tram engines; on 3 June 1891 John Thomas Hirst was killed at Crosland Moor, Huddersfield, when the engine he was driving exploded. The locomotive involved was No 9 in the fleet; it was six-years old and had been built to the Wilkinson Patent by Black Hawthorn of Gateshead. His death was marked by the composition of a 12-verse poem by William Hurst; two of the verses gave an accurate report of the accident:

For the boiler burst and all around
The fragments lay upon the ground;
Like a vessel dashed before the gale,
The engine was thrown clear off the rails.

A man, whose name was 'John Thomas Hirst,'
Was learning to drive when the boiler burst;
Away it sped, as though by fate 'twas led,
An now he's numbered with the silent dead.

Steam Tram Operations

It has been said that the steam tram was a very ephemeral form of transport having its heyday only from 1880 to 1905, but conversely, although operating over a far greater overall route mileage, horse trams did not carry anything like the number of passengers per route mile, and although starting earlier — 1875 for many — they finished quite precipitously once electric cars became possible, despite a rise in mileage from 237 (381km) in 1878 to 938 (1,509km) 20 years later.

The steam tram was in essence a small tank engine towing, and dwarfed by, a 70+seat trailer, normally double-deck with staircases at each end. Ideally, and unlike the successor electric cars, the two saloons were entirely enclosed, although here the Board of Trade inspectors had a frisson of doubt and required two or more windows upstairs to be omitted on narrow-gauge (3ft 6in) cars to reduce the risk of their being blown over in strong gales.

The Board of Trade Inspectors of Railways were to stultify the growth and conduct of steam trams on the roads of the British mainland and yet all their actions were taken with the best intentions. Believe it or not, one problem with these trams was their 'uncanny silence', simply because in any urban district you lived amid the noise of children, people in clogs on cobbles, iron-shod carts and waggons and machinery for many of the population lived cheek-by-jowl with factories and mills. And sometimes we get a terrible feeling today of déja vu; football supporters took subscription tickets and gave them to a local vicar to give to the 'deserving poor', each ticket being worth a 4lb (1.82kg) loaf, 4oz of tea, 1lb of sugar and 8oz of bacon; free school meals were the norm in Dudley 1888: 'a pint of good wholesome soup and a huge slice of bread and jam' were provided. And tram crews could find, despite all their hours work, that life could be fairly awful; from the 1891 census comes the following: 'Tram engine driver, 9 persons, three rooms. House dirty in the extreme. Ceilings almost black. Wall-paper infested and begrimed by smoke and dirt. One tap down the passage for 8 dwellings, area saturated with drainage from nearby stable.'

The Engineer, then and now a leading magazine in this field, carried a pertinent article in 1876, part of which reads: 'It is worth notice that the present movement in favour of steam tram cars owes its success to the labours of professional engineers ... and engineer takes a small railway locomotive, fits it with an apparatus for condensing steam, boxes it up to please the aesthetic taste of horses, and achieves almost by the turn of his hand a very large measure of success. It is difficult, indeed, to see why steam should not be used successfully on a tramway; and the failure of

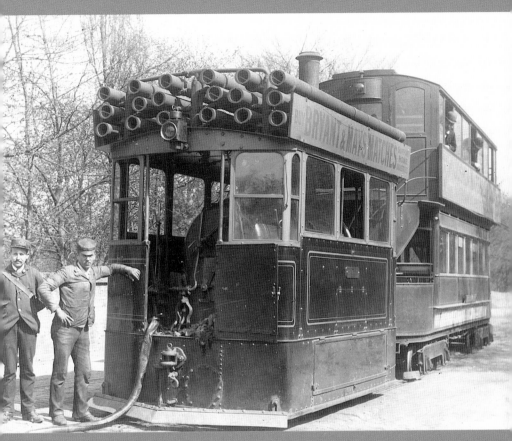

Nos 19 and 20 were built by Thos Green & Son and delivered to Huddersfield Corporation Tramways in 1891. These were excellent vehicles, albeit rather heavy on coke apparently; as compound working was unusually employed, they were driven by hand-picked drivers. Cylinders were 9 x 14in on the high-pressure side and 14 x 14in on the low. The tubes on the roof are Blackburn designed; these involved passing the steam from cylinders, etc through pipes inside these annular tubes — probably the most efficient design ever. The trailer was built by Geo F Milnes. Lifeguards are fitted to the engine and to the trailer, although the latter were rarely photographed, and the engine is here being watered.

an engineer thus to succeed might be regarded as abnormal. The mechanical difficulties involved are very trifling, and easily overcome; and we believe nothing is wanted but a little energy and caution on the part of the mechanical engineers to render the adoption of steam tram cars almost universal … .'

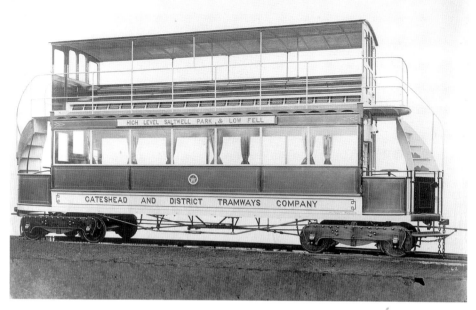

Brand new and gleaming, this Gateshead & District Tramways Co trailer is very skeletal but, like many others of the period, was designed to weigh under four English tons. The details are fascinating: the longitudinal 'outside' seating; the lack of 'decency' (advertising) boards; safety staircases; and, mohair curtains (these were soon dispensed with as they became infested). Built and supplied by the Falcon Engine & Car Co in 1883, later illustrations show this class of vehicle as having a slotted-in cover upstairs, decency boards and other changes. The dimensions were 19ft 4in in length (27ft 6in over the buffers), 5ft 4½in in width and 13ft 0in in height; seating capacity was 52.

But and but and but ... why did this story go largely pear shaped? First of all *The Engineer* again supplied a set of empirical figures in which it calculated the minimum weight of a tram engine, even with a four-ton trailer carrying 30 passengers (a two-horse load), would have to be four tons, giving a total of eight for the ensemble. But the rolling resistance of a small bogie car with plain bearings with a bare 2in springing stands at about 1,200lb and that on clean rails in good condition. If you add in the fact that inclines of 5% (1:20) were almost commonplace the theoretical basic figure of 7.4hp applying to ordinary railway tank engines becomes a nonsense. And there were and are two other problems that mechanically affect the design of road using tram engines. It was a legal requirement that they must not emit steam in any form — whether from the cylinders, the chimney or the escape valves — and this, therefore, had to be condensed — turned back into water — in a holding tank, but the boiler had to be kept full of water to function, and it is an unfortunate law of physics that, when this condensed water gets too hot (above 180°F/82°C), it cannot be reused in the boiler but instead has to be dumped down a convenient drain, and,

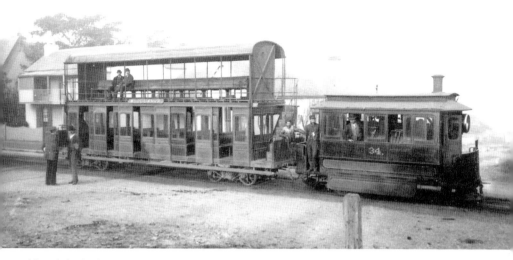

Although this book concentrates on British tramways, it is well worth looking over our shoulders at practice elsewhere given the importance of British influence on its Empire and other countries. This is Woollahra, a suburb of Sydney in Australia, on a line that opened on 17 May 1881. The line closed in 1895, still steam hauled, having been superseded by a cable line to Edgecliff. The trailer shows how loading was accelerated into the saloon, the sliding doors being useful in keeping out the worst of the city's storms. The use of double-deck trailers did not long outlast the steam-hauled services, being replaced by fast moving single-deck power cars and trailers, although collecting the fares from the side footboards could prove fatal to the conductors as they were hit by oncoming traffic. The knifeboard seating, the stairs and the double-entry upstairs on this trailer are reminiscent of the earliest tramcars supplied to UK operators. After the failure of underpowered British engines, power units came from the Baldwin Locomotive Works, Philadelphia.

in any event, will contain a surprising amount of 'foreign' matter picked up in its passage around the engine's workings. A tram engine in good fettle will need to produce and use 50lb of steam per horsepower per hour on average; therefore, the engine tanks must hold 280gall (1,275-litres) for each hour's working. The water in itself weighs 1.25 tons. In practice, with good design and a careful engine man as well as the reuse of some degree of condensate, a 2-2½-hour round trip was attainable.

The second problem was the fuel used as this was almost invariably coke which, the by-product of the gas works, varied enormously in its quality and purity. Its great advantages were that it was smokeless and capable of a hard intense heat. The theory was that a low ash, low sulphur bituminous coal entered the gas works and, after treatment, from this came a domestic and industrial gas supply used to the extent that electricity is today. A good household would have gas wall lights, a height adjustable chandelier, plus a super modern gas cooker (and a slight, but

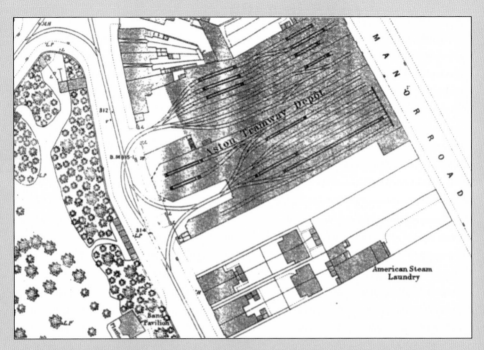

Tram Engines and trailers need to have somewhere to go for overnight storage. Even in the 1870s land in cities cost 'heavy' money but the Birmingham & Aston Tramways Co was able to build on what today would be known as a 'green field' site. The final depot to serve this site was, until recently, the home of the Aston Manor Road Transport Museum although the vicinity (within a few minutes walk from the Aston Villa football ground) has changed radically in 140 years.

pervasive smell of gas!) while outside the street lamps would all be gas fired. In any works, massive gas-powered furnaces would be roaring away, while the offices, too, would in the main have gas lights to brighten the grey Stygian fog of the evening. Left over from this vital form of heating and lighting were two by-products, in the form of a bituminous tar like compound, which was valuable, and gas-coke, which was only really fit for stoves, night-watchmen's braziers and the like — plus our tram engines. It will be understood the variation in quality was inherent in its origins, the basic coal could differ in quality even within one seam, the processing was extremely variable despite the best efforts of the gas works' engineers, and, while fresh coke held enough gas to be easily fired, after it had lain under snow or heavy rain it soaked up moisture by its porous nature, which not only short-changed the tram company as it was weighed by the ton, but the driver found himself with three or four sacks running with water and would have to nurse his fire thereafter. Add an indifferently steaming engine, plus the fact that the driver in early days at least could be nearing the end of his 12-14 hour day — seven days a week — with only such food as his wife or children could bring him, and it was little wonder time-keeping went completely out of the window.

Despite passenger demand, the ill-fated Dudley to Wolverhampton line had three owners during its brief life. Most of its problems could be blamed upon the demands of the tramway inspectorate. The line's first Act was obtained in 1880 but, after choosing the wrong pattern of rail and having its chosen engineer die on the job all the while fighting off the Inspector, it was not until 7 May 1883 that a sort of service — provided by horse tram — started. This two-hourly service required three horses for the hilly route, with the tramcar providing accommodation for 40 and, according to contemporary reports, operation over the 5½-mile route was 'erratic'. Even when steam cars ran, from 16 January 1886, their operation was constrained by their having to be only 5ft 6in in width as a result of the narrow streets through which the route operated. Kitson designed the locomotives and the trailers were supplied by Starbucks — delivered long before operation with them was possible; the latter seated a mere 54. The inside-framed bogies were designed to reduce overall width. *Alan Brotchie Collection*

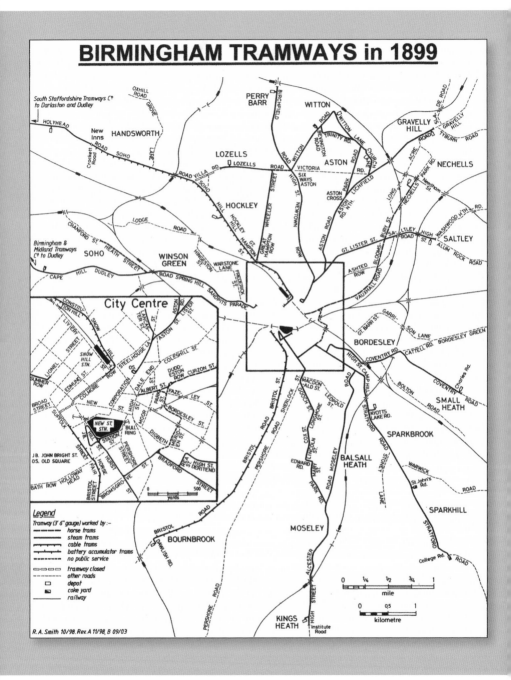

The details of any Tramway Order were complex and initially at least prohibited the company or the Corporation building the lines from actually operating the tramcars, but this rule rather fell apart in the case of Huddersfield where the Corporation having laid 10 miles or so of track could not find anyone to operate the cars — 'if the Corporation are unable to demise the tramways upon such terms as in the opinion of the Board of Trade shall yield the Corporation an adequate rent, the Board of Trade may grant a license to the Corporation to work such tramways' — although it did bolt on a clause that if after seven years someone else made a good offer the Corporation 'shall

The 3ft 6in Birmingham Central Tramways Co operated horse trams from 11 November 1884, steam trams from 25 November 1884, cable trams from 24 March 1888 and accumulator trams from 24 July 1890. The company was taken over by the City of Birmingham Tramways in October 1896. *Gerald Hartley*

demise said tramways to such company'. The original anti-monopoly clause (Standing Order 171 of 8 August 1878) became almost a dead letter as Plymouth and Blackpool (both 1892) Glasgow (1894) and Leeds (also 1894 but unofficially and probably without insurance) commenced operations, so two years later it was suspended.

The Central Tramways of Birmingham were unique in a number of aspects, not the least in that it operated four different systems of tramways simultaneously — steam, cable, horse and electric, although this latter was by accumulator (battery) cars. The then Borough, later City, Tramways Committee was very much on top of the tramways' problems; these included an omission which is almost inexplicable: the lack of any form of lifeguard on the engines — 'Your Committee have noticed with deep regret that during the past few months several fatal accidents have occurred on the tram lines within the Borough, from children being run over.' This was 4 October 1887 and contained a serious threat that, if steps were not taken to ameliorate the problem, then the permit to use steam would be withdrawn. We can see from the following statistics (a tiny percentage of those available thanks to the full reporting of the Birmingham Public Works Committee) that the costs of each type of transport varied enormously. In all 24.79 linear miles (39.89km) were operated by the company and, in the one year June 1891 to June 1892, its steam cars ran 1,212,624 miles, horse trams and omnibuses 634,551, cable cars 621,210 and electric 188,760. This resulted in the following figures:

	Average receipts per mile run	expenses pm	net profit pm
Steam	15.96d	12.03d	3.93d
Horse	11.20d	9.96d	1.24d
Cable	12.20d	6.18d	6.02d
Electric	13.25d	15.39d	2.14d (loss)

The following year, 1892/93, steam profits rose, horse fell, cable rose and the electric accumulator cars reduced their loss. Passenger numbers rose year-on-year from 22,182,041 in 1890 to 24,381,323 in the following year with each one paying 1.39d rising to 1.40d — each fare stage being normally one penny. Although individually the staff were hardly well paid, the total annual wage bill was £21,457. I should add here all these figures are in sterling and rather than confuse figures with conversions they can be best used in relation to one another, however one pound (£) = 240d.

Conversely, the Glasgow Tramway & Omnibus Co remained entirely horse drawn and in 1891 had 230 tramcars worth £17,250, 3,149 horses and mules worth £68,753, running roughly 5 million miles and carrying 52 million passengers.

But, finally, to revert to *The Engineer*, its editor had added a note of warning, which should perhaps have been noted by some of the overly optimistic promoters: 'Whether, in the long term they [steam trams] will in this country prove much cheaper than horse-worked cars we would not attempt to say.'

Dudley and Stourbridge
STEAM TRAMWAYS.

TIME TABLE.

HALF HOUR SERVICE, (except Sundays, also Saturday and Monday Afternoons.—See below.)

Cars leave Dudley Railway Station for Stourbridge every Hour and Half Hour from 7.30 a.m. to 9.30 p.m., passing through Dudley Market Place five minutes after each Hour and Half Hour; arriving at Stourbridge in half an hour from Brierley Hill and one hour from Dudley.

Cars leave Stourbridge for Dudley, ten minutes after each Hour and Half Hour from 8.40 a.m. to 10.40 p.m.; arriving at Dudley Railway Station in half an hour from Brierley Hill and in one hour from Stourbridge.

Sundays; also Saturday and Monday Afternoons.
Twenty Minutes Service.

Cars leave Dudley for Stourbridge at the Hour, and 20 minutes before and 20 minutes after the Hour, from 1.20 p.m. to 9.40 p.m. On Sundays:— Last Car leaves Dudley at 9.0 p.m.

Cars leave Stourbridge for Dudley at the Half Hour, and 10 minutes before and 10 minutes after the Hour, from 2.30 p.m. to 10.50 p.m. On Sundays :—Last Car leaves Stourbridge at 10.10 p.m.

South Staffordshire Steam Tramways.

Tram Cars leave the top of the Tipton Road, close to Dudley Railway Station about every Half Hour, for TIPTON, PRINCE'S END, DARLASTON, and WEDNESBURY.

Timetable for the Dudley and Stourbridge steam tramways.

The Barrow-in-Furness Tramways Co Ltd, latterly a subsidiary of British Electric Traction, operated steam trams over a 5½-mile 4ft 0in network between 11 July 1885 and 13 July 1903 when the route was electrified. *Gerald Hartley*

The Manchester, Bury, Rochdale & Oldham Steam Tramways Ltd operated a network of just under 31 route miles of which 9½ miles were standard gauge and the remainder 3ft 6in. In all the company employed 91 locomotives during is 21-year life with some 81 trailers. Engine No 84, a 3ft 6in gauge locomotive built by Beyer Peacock in 1886, is preserved by the National Tramway Museum but, is, at the time of writing, stored in a dismantled condition. *Gerald Hartley*

Opened on 20 September 1884 and operated until late 1893, the Coventry & District Tramways Co operated steam trams over a 3ft 6in gauge network of just over 13½ miles. Following closure, there was a gap of almost two years before electric trams commenced operation. *Gerald Hartley*

The Hartlepools Steam Tramways Co Ltd was financially unsuccessful. It opened its 3ft 6in gauge route on 2 August 1884 but was to close in 1891. It was not until five years later that a new electric tramway opened to serve the district. *Gerald Hartley*

One of the very few locations where standard (4ft 8½in) and narrow (3ft 6in) gauge steam tram engines could be seen side-by-side was Royton Yard, Dogford Road, of the Manchester, Bury, Rochdale & Oldham Steam Tramways Co. The roads of Rochdale were considered too narrow for the larger engines, whereas from Royton down the Oldham and Ashton roads the big Manning Wardles could tackle the gradients with ease, something that the narrow-gauge 'Wilkinson Pattern' engines seen here on the right could not have done. More than 100 years on Royton Yard still exists, albeit now in different ownership and without the trams.

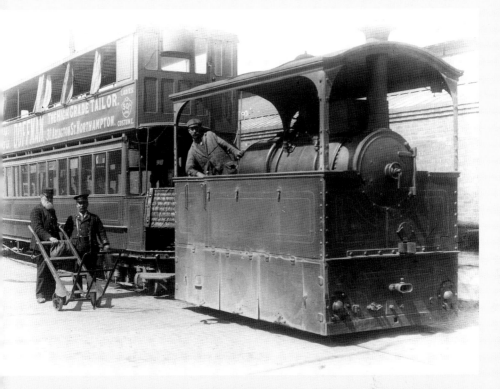

The author is not ashamed to admit that this symphony of men and machines is one of his favourite photographs. The tramway is the 3ft 6in Wolverton & Stony Stratford, which had the purpose of providing transport for workmen to the London & North Western Railway's carriage works at Wolverton as well as carrying 'working girls' to a nearby print works. The line, some 2⅝ miles in length on a slightly hilly route, opened on 27 May 1887; a short-lived extension, opened in 1888, took the line a further 2½ miles to Deanshanger. The first three locomotives were supplied by the Locomotivfabrik Krauss & Co of Sendling in Germany. The trio had the relatively high boiler pressure of 175psi and were fitted with 8 x 12in cylinders. Some idea of the work that they faced can be gauged from the size of the 44ft long, 100-seat trailer that was supplied by the Midland Carriage & Wagon Co. The line was acquired by the L&NWR in the early 1920s and passed to the LMSR in 1923; it closed three years later. The guard in the photograph was Billy Newton; unfortunately, the name of the bewhiskered L&NWR employee is unknown.

GREAT EASTERN RAILWAY

OPENING

OF THE

WISBECH & UPWELL

TRAMWAY

THROUGHOUT TO UPWELL

On MONDAY, 8th SEPTEMBER, 1884, the WISBECH & UPWELL TRAMWAY will be Open throughout to Upwell, and Tram Cars will run as under:—WEEK DAYS.

	a.m.	a.m.	a.m.	p.m.	p.m.	p.m.
Wisbech Station	6 45	9 15	11 40	2 15	5 10	7 50
Elm Bridge	7 3	9 35	12 0	2 33	5 28	8 8
Boyce's Bridge	7 17	9 50	12 15	2 47	5 42	8 22
Outwell Basin	7 25	10 0	12 25	2 55	5 50	8 30
Outwell Village	7 35	10 10	12 35	3 5	6 0	8 40
Upwell	7 45	10 20	12 45	3 15	6 10	8 50

	a.m.	a.m.	p.m.	p.m.	p.m.	p.m.
Upwell	7 55	10 30	12 55	3 40	6 35	9 0
Outwell Village	8 5	10 40	1 5	3 50	6 45	9 10
Outwell Basin	8 15	10 50	1 15	4 0	6 45	9 20
Boyce's Bridge	8 25	10 58	1 25	4 10	6 53	9 28
Elm Bridge	8 37	11 12	1 40	4 25	7 7	9 42
Wisbech Station	8 55	11 30	2 0	4 45	7 25	10 0

The Tram Cars will stop for the purpose of setting down or taking up Passengers at any point along the line of route.

FARES:—

	Wisbech.			
Elm Bridge	3d. 2d.			
Boyce's Bridge	3d. 2d.	3d. 2d.	Boyce's Bridge	
Outwell Basin	3d. 2d.	3d. 2d.	2d. 1d.	Outwell Basin
Outwell Village	4d. 3d.	3d. 2d.	3d. 2d.	2d. 1d.	Outwell Village
Upwell	4d. 3d.	4d. 3d.	3d. 2d.	3d. 2d.	2d. 1d.	2d. 1d.	Upwell

Personal Luggage not exceeding 56 lbs. in weight will be allowed to be taken by each Adult Passenger free of charge if carried by hand.

MERCHANDISE TRAFFIC

Will be dealt with at the following Sidings or Depots :—

ELM BRIDGE, BOYCE'S BRIDGE, OUTWELL BASIN, OUTWELL BRIDGE, UPWELL.

WILLIAM BIRT, General Manager

This trio of illustrations record a railway-pattern tramway — the Wisbech & Upwell Tramway — opened originally by the Great Eastern Railway on 8 September 1884. 'Limited to hauling 100 tons at 8mph … the engine has four wheels, is built light but powerful, the wheels being three feet in diameter. The steam pressure is almost noiseless, the steam being conveyed into condensing tanks holding 440 gallons of water. The whole of the engine is enclosed in a teak casing [which] gives it the appearance of an ordinary luggage van so that animals on the road may not be frightened by it.' The first of these illustrations shows the opening notice; the second records locomotive No 0125, which was designed by James Holden and built as one of a class of 12 constructed between 1903 and 1921 (No 0125 was actually one of those delivered in 1921 and was to survive as BR Class J70 No 68224 until March 1952); the same locomotive — but this time numbered simply 125 — stands with a tidy tram train. Passenger services over the line were withdrawn in 1927. The canal, part of which still existed at the time of writing, was the Wisbech, which was constructed under an Act of 1794 and officially abandoned in 1926; it was 5¼ miles in length.

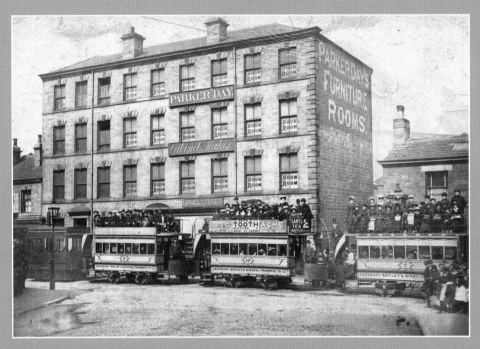

The Dewsbury, Batley & Birstal (sic) Tramways Co was a simple one operating between the three towns of its name, although it did open in stages: to Birstall by 1875 and to Gomersal in 1881. The locomotives chosen to operate the line were the relatively rare products of Merryweather & Co of Greenwich; these locomotives represented one of the best designs manufactured and may well have contributed to this line consistently paying dividends to its shareholders. This is clearly a demonstration view taken in Bradford Road, Dewsbury, as running more than one trailer was anathema to the Board of Trade; all three of the trailers illustrated were ex-horse trams and at least a couple of them survived to pass into British Electric Traction ownership.

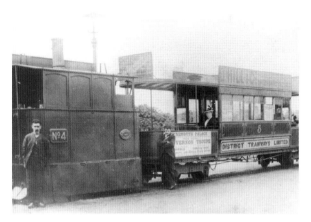

Contrary to appearances, this trailer is not a converted hen house but rather an ex-Metropolitan (London) horse tram converted by Charles Foote of Preston (North Shields) into a steam trailer for the North Shields District Tramway. The front and rear staircases along with the upper deck from the horse tram were removed, with the remainder of the body placed upon a new chassis, second-hand bogies and open platforms. Photographed in *circa* 1900, possibly in Percy Park, the whole ensemble looks shabby.

This delightful illustration depicts the Clogher Valley line in Caledon Town, coming up from Tynan. The 0-4-2 locomotive is No 1 *Caledon*, which was built by Sharp Stewart (Works' No 3369/1886). It had 13½ x 18in cylinders and, in contrast to 10-12 ton orthodox tram engines, weighed 23¾ tons. The 13 carriages came from the Metropolitan Railway Carriage & Wagon Co of Birmingham, as did six luggage-cum-brake vans and 74 goods wagons. Given the gradients along the line, it is hardly surprising that vacuum brakes were fitted to all rolling stock. The line closed in 1942. *Don Quail Collection*

Free from the dead hand of the Board of Trade, Irish tramways, even where they were recognisably primarily passenger lines, regarded freight as a vital part of their income, although this traffic was necessarily limited by the size of their engines. Ballygawley Fair was not a fair in the English sense but a 'beast' sales fair held on the second Friday of each month; markets for domestic produce, such as potatoes, oats, eggs and butter, were held each Friday. Situated in County Tyrone, Ballygowley had to wait for some years for modern transport as the building of the Clogher Valley Tramway was a protracted affair, with the 3ft 0in gauge line not opening until 1887. Tynan provided a connection with the GNR(I) and Auchnacloy was the headquarters of the company. Despite later becoming the Clogher Valley Railway and hunting for any available traffic, the line required subsidy in all but one year during its life until closure in 1942.

CLOGHER VALLEY TRAMWAY.

BALLYGAWLEY FAIR.

A Special Train will leave Ballygawley for Tynan at 2-20 p.m. Cattle for shipment by that train must be loaded up not later than 2-0 p.m.

D. J STEWART,
General Manager.

AUGHNACLOY,
9th June, 1892.

W. Somers, Printer, Aughnacloy.

The Giant's Causeway, Portrush & Bush Valley Railway & Tramway Co was a little tramway with a spectacularly long name! As the important part of the story lay in the use by the Siemens Brothers of a hydro-electric scheme, the story of the line's electrification will be told in the author's companion volume on early electric tramways, suffice to record here that, initially at least, steam was used as a back-up although the six-mile route seems to have been well served by steam. In 1897, the four Wilkinson engines ran a total of 17,797 miles, with only 4,721 miles run by the electric cars. As time went on, however, the figures changed, so that in 1913 37,238 miles were operate by electric traction but only 3,863 by steam. The line was first inspected on 12 January 1883 and was to close finally on 1 October 1949. This photograph, taken at the Causeway terminus, shows the glory of No 1 *Dunluce Castle* in its livery of Tuscan Red and cream at the head of a typical summer service train.

Castle Hill, Dudley, at the point where, today, the A461 meets the A4037 on the right. Dudley Castle is just discernible in the centre background whilst a steam tram and trailer of the Dudley & Stourbridge stands on the far side of the bridge over the L&NWR line from Walsall to Stourbridge. Apart from a single horse and cart, traffic at this now important intersection is conspicuous by its absence.

It's Spring Bank, Pemberton, and, in 1903, a passenger alights from a Wigan & District Tramways Co engine and trailer. Looking down the hill, the normal murk of Wigan is obvious and it seems that villas were built up here to allow residents to enjoy the relatively clean air.

A busy view of the south end of Stockton High Street in the 1890s. Occupied premises include R Goodson (Paraffin and Gas Mantle Manufacturers), the 'Exchange Dining Rooms', Stewart's the clothiers, and A & G Taylor, whose premises over 106 High Street, Stockton (occupied 1880-1911) gave them an excellent viewpoint for their business as photographers. It is assumed that one of their staff took this photograph.

End of the line and transition

The death knell for both for both horse and steam trams came with the development of electric traction. The early years of electric tramways are discussed more fully in the author's companion volume on early electric tramways but suffice here to note that experimentation in the use of electricity in transport occurred at the same time as both horse and steam trams were being developed. The first permanent tramway to use electric power supplied by an overhead wire was in a suburb of Berlin in 1880. It was not long before electric traction reached the British Isles. In 1883, Magnus Volk opened his 2ft 0in gauge line along the seafront in Brighton and, two years later on 29 September 1885, the pioneer of electric tramways in Britain, Michael Holroyd Smith, introduced his first tramway in Blackpool — a conduit line along the Promenade.

These developments in England coincided with the construction of two pioneering electric lines in Ireland: the Giant's Causeway tramway, which eventually linked Portrush with the Giant's Causeway on the Antrim coast, first used electric traction on 28 September 1883 whilst the Bessbrook & Newry, which linked the Great Northern Railway (Ireland) station at Newry with Bessbrook, saw public services introduced on 1 October 1885. In Leeds, commencing on 29 October 1891, an experimental route using conventional overhead was launched by the American Thomson-Houston Co whilst, in neighbouring Bradford, the enterprising Holroyd Smith demonstrated the potential of electric trams on a short route up Cheapside in March 1892.

Electric traction offered many advantages. For horse tram operators it meant the end of the need to recruit, feed and house large numbers of horses whilst for steam tram operators it reduced the dirt and noise that were associated with the operation of steam trams. By the late 19th century another facet was coming into play. Whilst Huddersfield had been a pioneer of municipal operation, even after the Corporation undertook its own operations in 1883 most new tram systems were still company operated. It was at the end of the licence periods, as catered for under the 1870 Act, that many local authorities took control. Municipal operation was a source of considerable local pride, just as it was in terms of the municipal ownership of the gas works, electricity power station, and the water and sewerage systems. Although many of the municipal operators inherited steam or horse tramways, they were generally quick to convert these lines to electric traction. Moreover, in those towns that did not succumb to municipal operation, companies such as British Electric Traction were equally keen to bring the benefits of this new form of power to passengers.

In June 1900, to mark the end of the steam tram in the district, all the people with the slightest connection with Blackburn Corporation and other local tramways made the journey from Darwen to Bacup in Lancashire, via Haslingden, Rawtenstall and Waterfoot — a feat of endurance lasting four-and-a-half hours. Lunch was taken at the Commercial Hotel, Accrington, where this view was taken. *Jim Halsall Collection*

The operation of Heywood Corporation's steam tramway was to be one of the shortest ever and resulted from the electrification of the lines from Rochdale and Bury to the boundaries of Heywood. The three councils — all very parochial — had argued over the cost of installing the overhead and relaying the track with the result that Heywood — as successor to the Manchester, Bury, Rochdale & Oldham Steam Tramways Co — continued to operate steam trams, running the service from 20 December 1904 to 20 September 1905. The steam trams were replaced by the electric cars of Bury Corporation. Here, inside the 'temporary' shed, the last rites are carried out as both locomotives and trailers are dismantled.

From the late 19th century onwards, and particularly in the first decade of the 20th, horse and steam trams rapidly disappeared. Not all were replaced by electric trams; the horse tramways in Oxford and Cambridge were replaced by early petrol buses as the city fathers rejected the unsightly overhead wires whilst the horse trams in Douglas, on the Isle of Man, have never been replaced (although there were plans in the early 20th century to see the route along the promenade electrified). The last steam tramways to operate in Britain were both railway owned and never electrified. The Wolverton & Stony Stratford, by now controlled by the London, Midland & Scottish Railway, last ran on 19 May 1926 whilst the London & North Eastern Railway withdrew passenger services on the Wisbech & Upwell on 1 January 1928 due to bus competition. The latter line, however, continued to carry freight traffic until final closure on 23 May 1966.

An interesting transitional view: the steam trams in Coventry seem to have been fairly awful as they were underpowered for the work and the one better, if second-hand, Falcon engine had been used for all manner of experiments by its previous owner. A contemporary reports notes that after three failed attempts to climb the hill at Bishop Street an engine and trailer set back, were uncoupled whilst No 7, the Falcon, was sent for; the report continues 'eventually up came another engine, much bigger and heavier, its sides loose and making a terrible noise. It was kept for this special rescue service ... steam was got up amid clouds of more black smoke and clunk, clunk, clunk once more.' It finally made it but, with the failed efforts, the $5\frac{3}{8}$-mile journey to Bedworth took from 4.30pm to 10pm. Unsurprisingly the new Coventry Electric Tramways Co Ltd was quick to move to electric cars and purchased four from Brush in 1895, said to be for quick delivery tacked on to an order for Rouen in France. As can be seen, they were primitive but the trailer used here was No 9, one of the steam tram trailers supplied by Falcon in 1884 and still retaining its plate frame bogies. The photograph dates to between December 1895, when No 1 was delivered, and 1898, when No 9 was converted to an electric car.

It is to be wondered whether the photographer had any inkling of how important this panoramic view of Briggate in Leeds would become as a record of the transition from steam to electric traction. The first electric trams in Leeds were towed — by a steam tram engine! — on 17 July 1897 with the last steam trams operating in the city in December 1901.

With work on the construction of the London County Council's conduit electric trams in the foreground, LCC horse tram No 827, based at Clapham Depot, is pictured on the long route from Clapham Common to Waterloo station. The complexity of installing the electric conduit system is all too evident in the view.

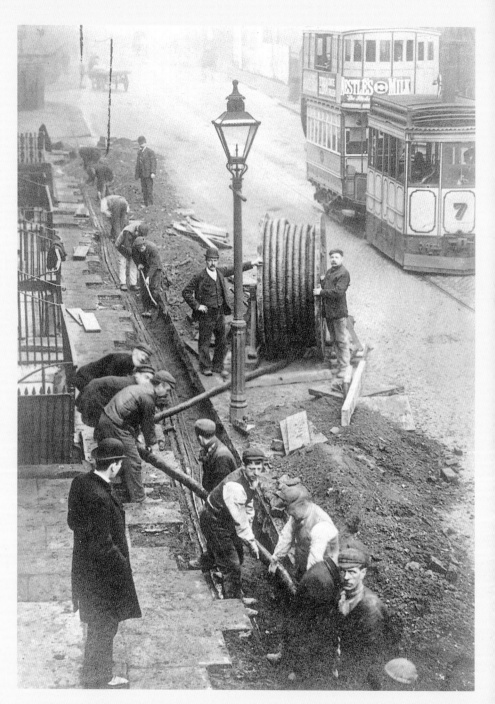

Dundee Corporation trailer No 4 stands with the overhead for the electric trams *in situ*; this probably dates the photograph to *circa* 1900. The steam trams finished in the city on 14 May 1902. The locomotive was a product of Thos Green & Co; it is notable for the later pattern condenser, which was much more efficient that the earlier transverse arrangement. *Alan Brotchie Collection*

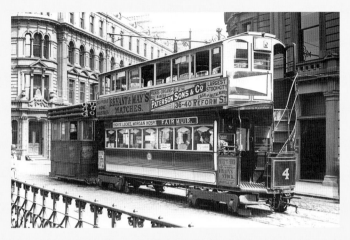

The first de Dion-Bouton tricycles to be manufactured commercially appeared in 1896, a decade after Karl Benz produced the first patented motorcar using an internal combustion engine, although steam-operated 'drags' (a form of bus) hold been sold in 1893. This illustration, from a catalogue produced in 1898, shows a motor-drag or articulated bus although it is uncertain if it operated. If it had, engine unreliability and poor braking would have been problems, but improvements in the technology of both would lead to the demise of most surviving horse and steam tramways as well as many of the country's electric tramways.

Opposite: Probably a deliberately posed view, this records the electrification of Bradford Road — part of the Dewsbury, Batley & Birstal tramway — in 1905. All the components of the interloper are there, but No 7 (Merryweather Works' No 118/1881) and trailer (probably the rebuilt No 6 of 1880) are still clean and smart in their improbable yellow livery. The electric cable is wrapped in gutta-percha — a natural inert latex — to protect against the ingress of damp. *Geoff Lumb Collection*

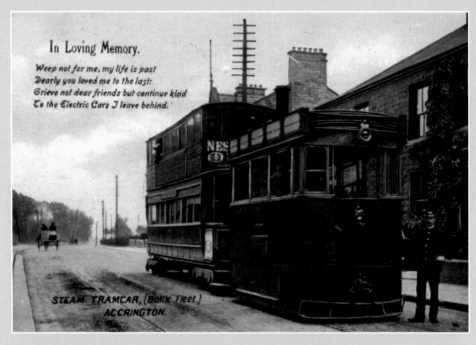

In Loving Memory.

Weep not for me, my life is past
Dearly you loved me to the last:
Grieve not dear friends but continue kind
To the Electric Cars I leave behind.

STEAM TRAMCAR, (Baltic Fleet.)
ACCRINGTON.

Above: How far this was true is anyone's guess, but the text on this card, which was posted from Accrington on 26 December 1907, indicates either someone was sentimental or saw a way of using up a stock of cards. Accrington's venture into steam tram operation was one of the most successful, overcoming an unusual form of experimental trackwork and the subsequent bankruptcy of the main contractor. Under the auspices of a private company the first commercial services ran on 5 April 1886; subsequently taken over by the local authority, steam services ceased on 31 December 1907. The engine visible here is a 'standard' Thomas Green of Leeds product with the trailer being built by the Ashbury Railways Carriage & Iron Co. The first electric cars operated on 2 August 1907, albeit on different routes, giving some overlap.

Epilogue: If we assume that even inanimate objects have souls then tramcars, buses and trains must have very powerful ones otherwise why would otherwise sane people restore rusting hulks back to a condition probably better than when they were new? By they do and let us be thankful. Neither item here survived to the 21st century but one wonders what the lower deck of a Bury, Rochdale & Oldham steam tram trailer, serving as a shelter at New Hey, thought as it watched Rochdale Corporation No 35 — a Brush 'Combination' car delivered in 1905 — pass by. A very satisfying final photograph.

Opposite bottom: Some companies began their services in almost an apologetic manner, quietly starting on the one more-or-less completed route, whereas a municipal operator liked a bit of a show — this, they said, is what your rates have paid for. And, given the brightness of the cars against the gas lamps normally in use, their speed against walking, and their relative quietness, small wonder there was pride. This card was posted at 12.30pm in Newcastle on 4 January 1905 to an address in Darlington and, as can be seen, commemorates the opening of the latter's tramways to Harrowgate Hill, Eastbourne and Barton Street by the Lady Mayoress, Mrs A Henderson, and the Town Clerk's wife, Mrs J Wilkes, on 1 January. Three trams are visible, all from the first batch (Nos 1-16) delivered from Milnes in 1903 to a very German pattern of combination saloon with only two windows and open smokers' sections at each end. They were fitted with McGuire trucks and Westinghouse equipment, already somewhat outmoded. The Darlington system lasted until 10 April 1926, when the trams were replaced on vastly extended routes by trolleybuses.

Index